PIANO · VOCAL · GUITAR

THE BEST SHOWTUNES EVER

SHOW TUNES

ISBN 978-1-4803-4015-2

HAL·LEONARD®
CORPORATION

7777 W. BLUEMOUND RD. P.O. BOX 13819 MILWAUKEE, WI 53213

Visit Hal Leonard Online at
www.halleonard.com

ABOUT A QUARTER TO NINE
from 42ND STREET

Lyrics by AL DUBIN
Music by HARRY WARREN

AIN'T MISBEHAVIN'
from AIN'T MISBEHAVIN'

Words by ANDY RAZAF
Music by THOMAS "FATS" WALLER
and HARRY BROOKS

for, be - lieve me. I don't stay out late,

don't care to go, I'm home a - bout eight, just me and my ra - di - o.

Ain't mis - be - hav - in', I'm sav - in' my love for you.

you.

THE BEST THINGS IN LIFE ARE FREE

from GOOD NEWS!

Music and Lyrics by B.G. DeSYLVA,
LEW BROWN and RAY HENDERSON

ALL OF YOU
from SILK STOCKINGS

Words and Music by
COLE PORTER

e - ven the heart and soul of you. So love at least a small per - cent of me, do, for I love all of you. I love the you.

AQUARIUS
from the Broadway Musical Production HAIR

Words by JAMES RADO and GEROME RAGNI
Music by GALT MacDERMOT

BIDIN' MY TIME

from GIRL CRAZY

Music and Lyrics by GEORGE GERSHWIN
and IRA GERSHWIN

BILL
from SHOW BOAT

Music by JEROME KERN
Words by P.G. WODEHOUSE
and OSCAR HAMMERSTEIN II

BUT NOT FOR ME
from GIRL CRAZY

Music and Lyrics by GEORGE GERSHWIN
and IRA GERSHWIN

BUTTON UP YOUR OVERCOAT

from FOLLOW THRU

Words and Music by B.G. DeSYLVA,
LEW BROWN and RAY HENDERSON

CAN'T HELP LOVIN' DAT MAN

from SHOW BOAT

Lyrics by OSCAR HAMMERSTEIN II
Music by JEROME KERN

Oh lis-ten, sis-ter, I love my Mis-ter man ____ and I can't ____ tell yo' why. ____ Dere ain't no rea-son why I should love dat man. ____ It must be sump-in' dat ____

DANCING ON THE CEILING

from SIMPLE SIMON
from EVERGREEN

Words by LORENZ HART
Music by RICHARD RODGERS

DANCE ONLY WITH ME

from SAY, DARLING

Music by JULE STYNE
Words by BETTY COMDEN and ADOLPH GREEN

DAY BY DAY
from the Musical GODSPELL

Music by STEPHEN SCHWARTZ
Lyrics by RICHARD OF CHICHESTER (1197-1253)

DEFYING GRAVITY
from the Broadway Musical WICKED

Music and Lyrics by
STEPHEN SCHWARTZ

Freely, with quiet intensity

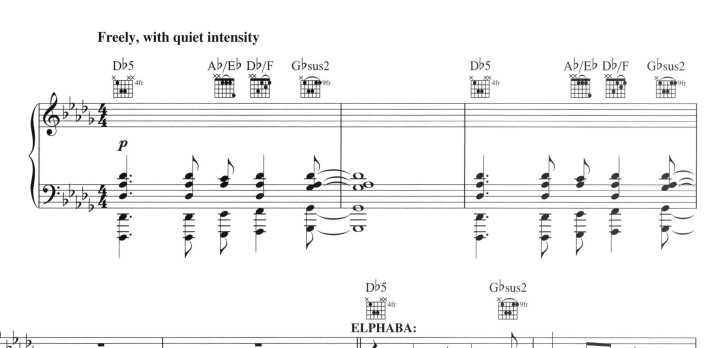

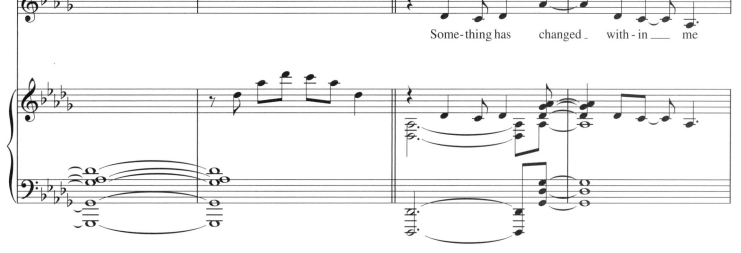

ELPHABA:

Some-thing has changed _ with-in _ me

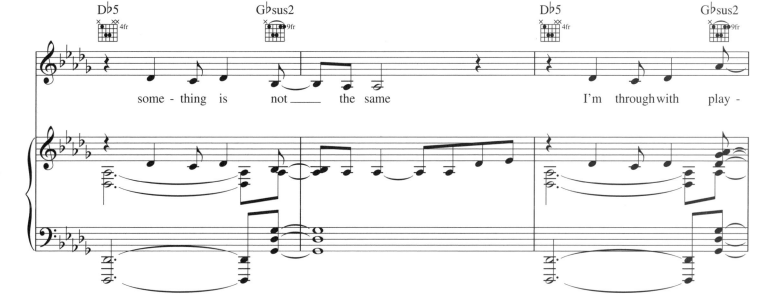

some-thing is not ___ the same   I'm through with play -

all of Oz, no Wiz-ard that there is or was is ev-er gon-na

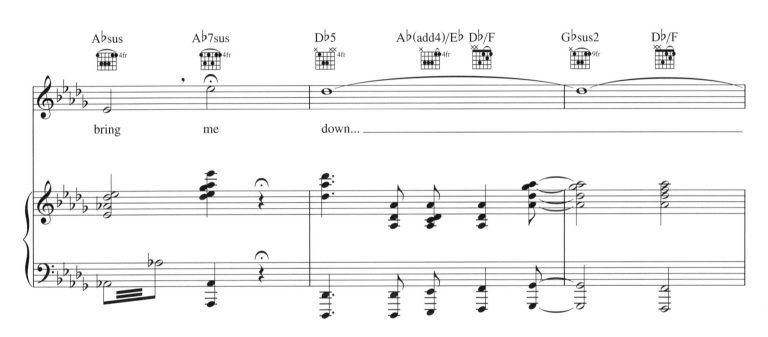

bring me down... Ah!

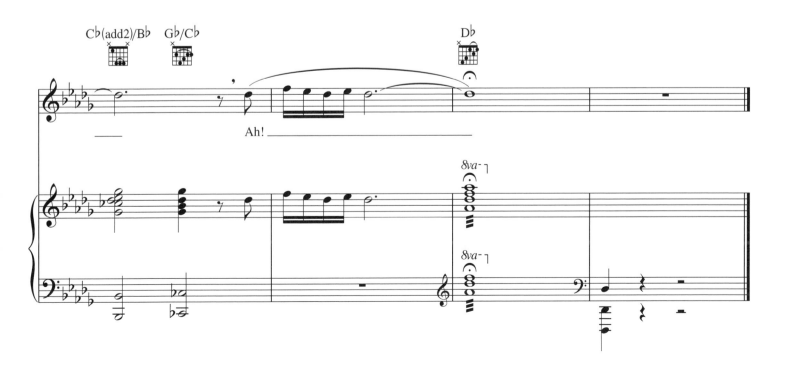

DO YOU HEAR THE PEOPLE SING?

from LES MISÉRABLES

Music by CLAUDE-MICHEL SCHÖNBERG
Lyrics by ALAIN BOUBLIL, JEAN-MARC NATEL
and HERBERT KRETZMER

song of an - gry men? It is the mu - sic of a peo - ple who will not be slaves a- gain! When the

beat - ing of your heart ech-oes the beat - ing of the drums, there is a life a-bout to start when to-mor - row

FEUILLY:

comes! Will you life a-bout to start when to-mor - row comes!

FASCINATING RHYTHM

from the Broadway Musical LADY, BE GOOD!

Music and Lyrics by GEORGE GERSHWIN
and IRA GERSHWIN

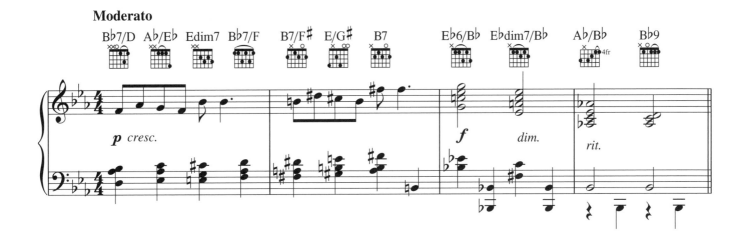

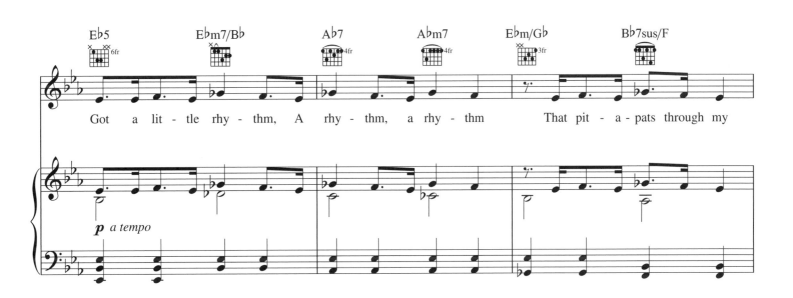

Got a lit-tle rhy-thm, A rhy-thm, a rhy-thm That pit-a-pats through my

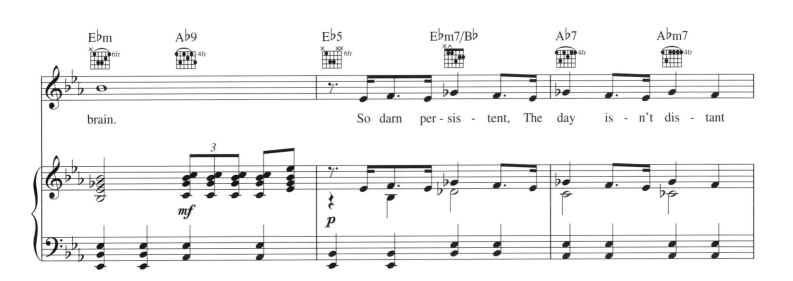

brain. So darn per-sis-tent, The day is-n't dis-tant

DOWN WITH LOVE
from the Musical Production HOORAY FOR WHAT!

Lyric by E.Y. "YIP" HARBURG
Music by HAROLD ARLEN

EASTER PARADE
from AS THOUSANDS CHEER

Words and Music by
IRVING BERLIN

EMBRACEABLE YOU

from CRAZY FOR YOU

Music and Lyrics by GEORGE GERSHWIN
and IRA GERSHWIN

EV'RY TIME WE SAY GOODBYE

from SEVEN LIVELY ARTS

Words and Music by
COLE PORTER

FEELING GOOD

from THE ROAR OF THE GREASEPAINT—THE SMELL OF THE CROWD

Words and Music by LESLIE BRICUSSE
and ANTHONY NEWLEY

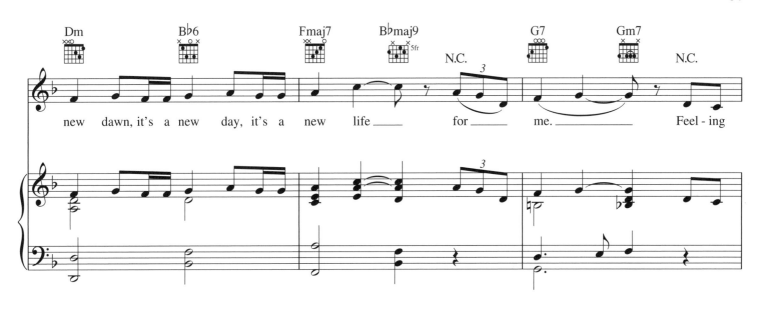

new dawn, it's a new day, it's a new life _____ for _____ me. _____ Feel - ing

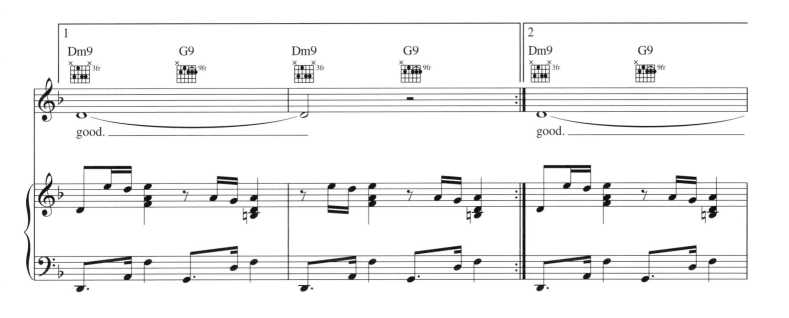

good. _____ good. _____

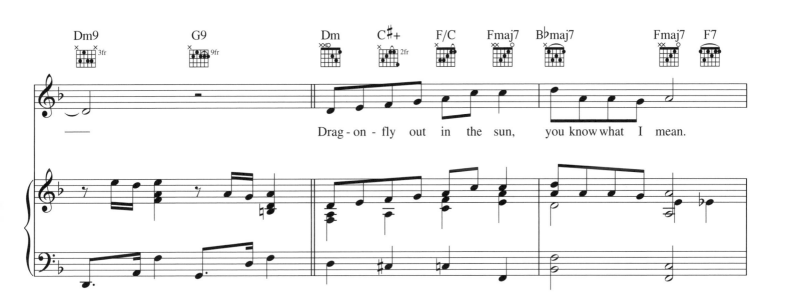

_____ Drag - on - fly out in the sun, you know what I mean.

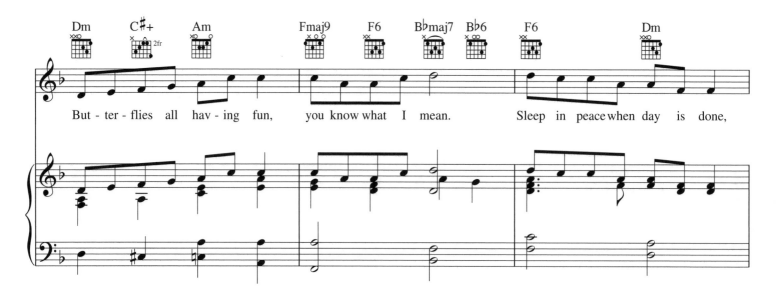

But - ter - flies all hav - ing fun, you know what I mean. Sleep in peace when day is done,

that's what I mean. ___ And this old world is a new world and a bold world ___ for ___

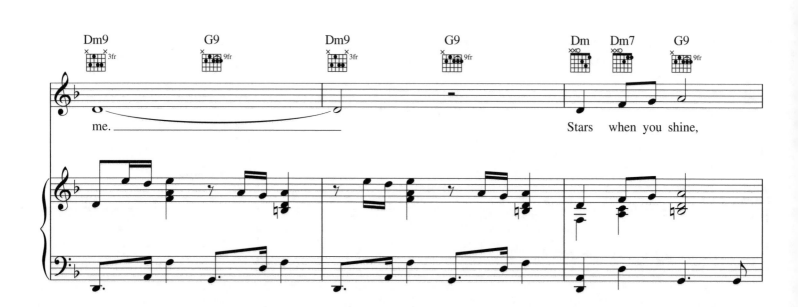

me. ___ Stars when you shine,

FORTY-SECOND STREET

from 42ND STREET

Words by AL DUBIN
Music by HARRY WARREN

GLAD TO BE UNHAPPY

from ON YOUR TOES

Words by LORENZ HART
Music by RICHARD RODGERS

Reflectively

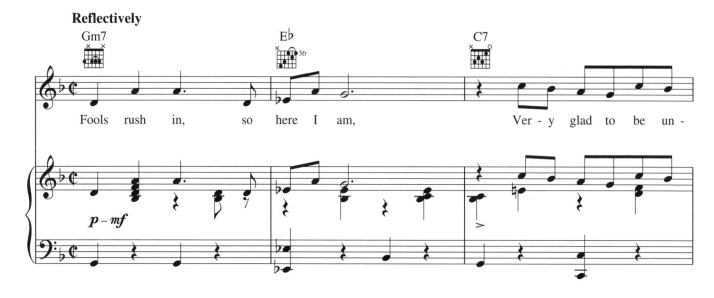

Fools rush in, so here I am, Ver - y glad to be un-

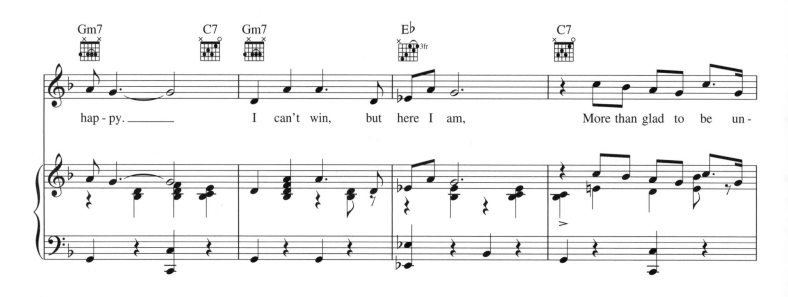

hap - py. _____ I can't win, but here I am, More than glad to be un-

hap - py. _____ Un - re - quit - ed love's a bore, And I've got it pret - ty

GOOD MORNING STARSHINE

from the Broadway Musical Producion HAIR

Words by JAMES RADO and GEROME RAGNI
Music by GALT MacDERMOT

Repeat and Fade

HE LOVES AND SHE LOVES

from FUNNY FACE

Music and Lyrics by GEORGE GERSHWIN
and IRA GERSHWIN

107

HERNANDO'S HIDEAWAY
from THE PAJAMA GAME

Words and Music by RICHARD ADLER
and JERRY ROSS

Lyrics: I know a dark se-clud-ed place, a place where no one knows your face. A glass of wine a

HEY THERE
from THE PAJAMA GAME

Words and Music by RICHARD ADLER
and JERRY ROSS

I CAN'T GET STARTED
from ZIEGFELD FOLLIES

Words by IRA GERSHWIN
Music by VERNON DUKE

HOW LONG HAS THIS BEEN GOING ON?

from ROSALIE

Music and Lyrics by GEORGE GERSHWIN
and IRA GERSHWIN

Bill: As a tot, when I trot-ted in lit-tle vel-vet pant - ies, _____
Mary: 'Neath the stars, at ba-zaars, of - ten I've had to ca-ress men. _____

I was kissed by my sis-ters, my cous-ins and my aunt - ies. _____
Five or ten dol-lars, then, I'd col-lect from all those yes - men. _____

Sad to tell, it was Hell, an in-fer-no worse than Dan - te's. _____
Don't be sad; I must add that they meant no more than chess - men. _____

I DON'T KNOW HOW TO LOVE HIM

from JESUS CHRIST SUPERSTAR

Words by TIM RICE
Music by ANDREW LLOYD WEBBER

I GOT PLENTY O' NUTTIN'

from PORGY AND BESS®

Music and Lyrics by GEORGE GERSHWIN,
DuBOSE and DOROTHY HEYWARD
and IRA GERSHWIN

I GOT RHYTHM

from AN AMERICAN IN PARIS
from GIRL CRAZY

Music and Lyrics by GEORGE GERSHWIN
and IRA GERSHWIN

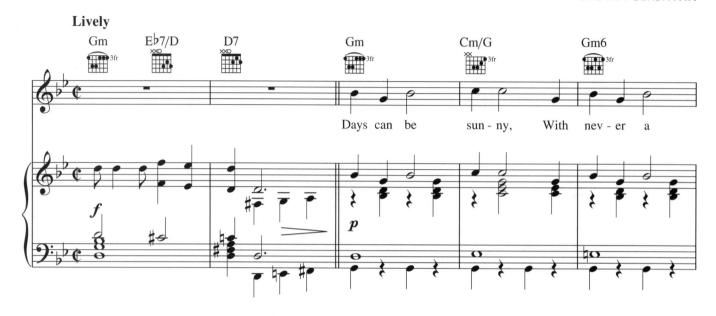

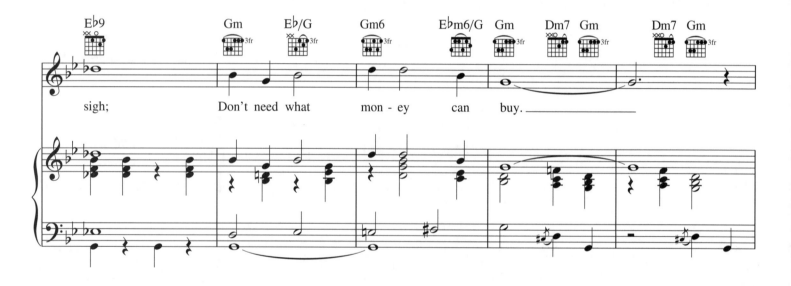

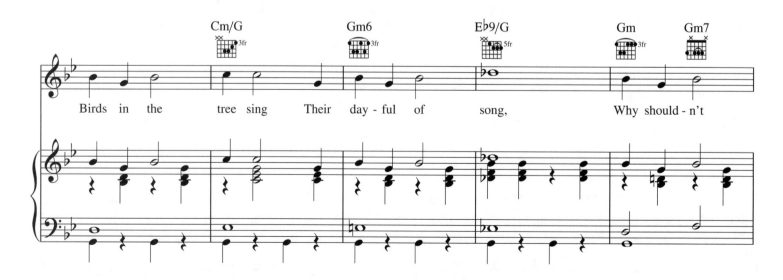

I LOVE PARIS

from CAN-CAN
from HIGH SOCIETY

Words and Music by
COLE PORTER

I ONLY HAVE EYES FOR YOU

from DAMES

Words by AL DUBIN
Music by HARRY WARREN

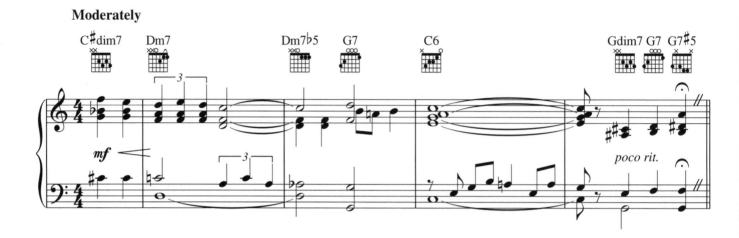

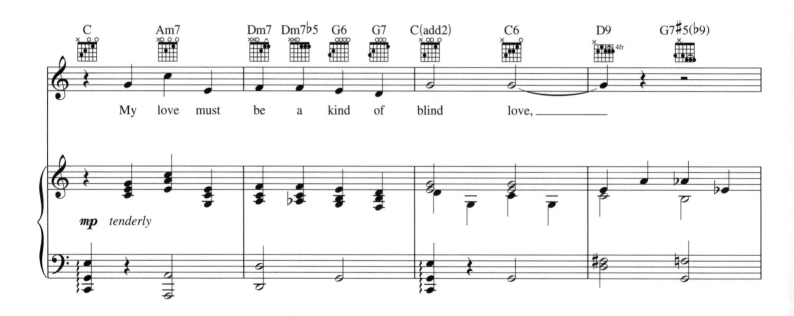

My love must be a kind of blind love,

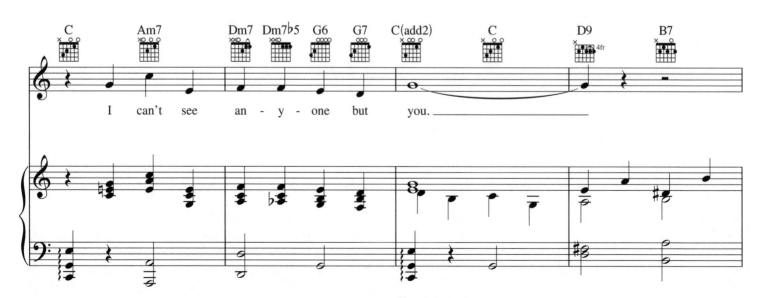

I can't see an-y-one but you.

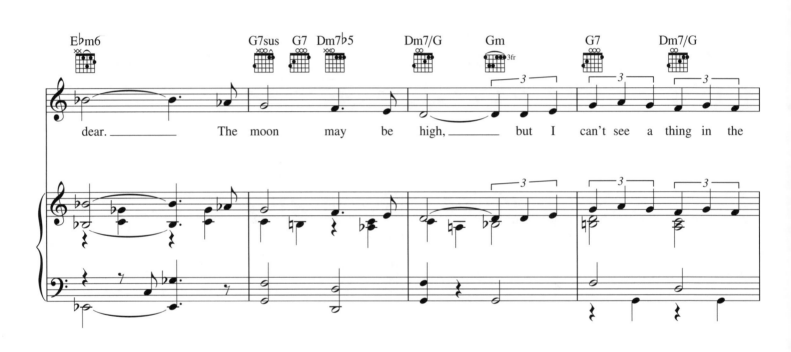

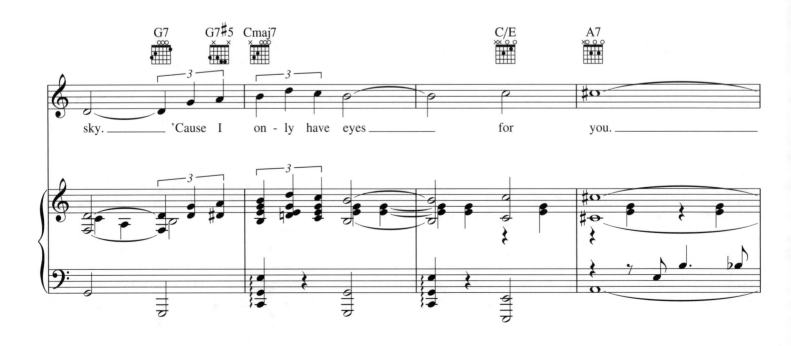

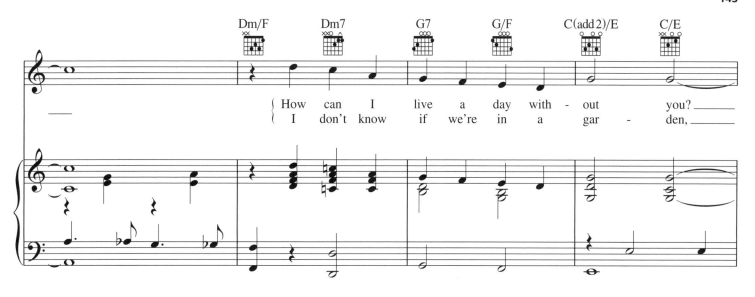

How can I live a day with - out you? _____
I don't know if we're in a gar - den, _____

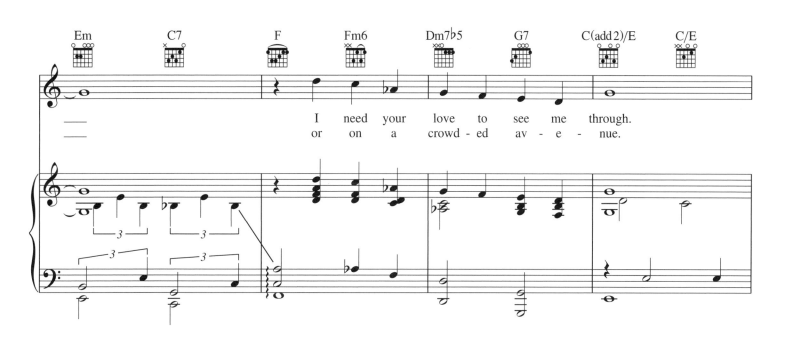

I need your love to see me through.
or on a crowd - ed av - e - nue.

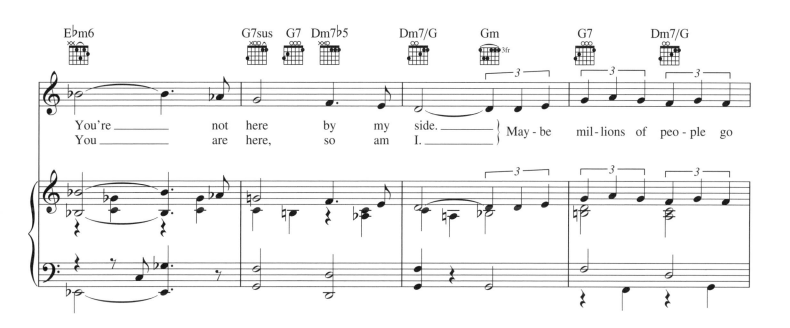

You're _____ not here by my side. _____
You _____ are here, so am I. _____
May - be mil - lions of peo - ple go

by. _____ But they all dis - ap - pear _____ from

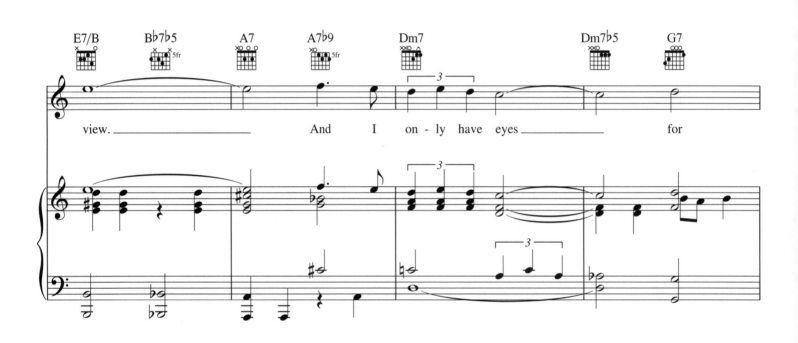

view. _____ And I on - ly have eyes _____ for

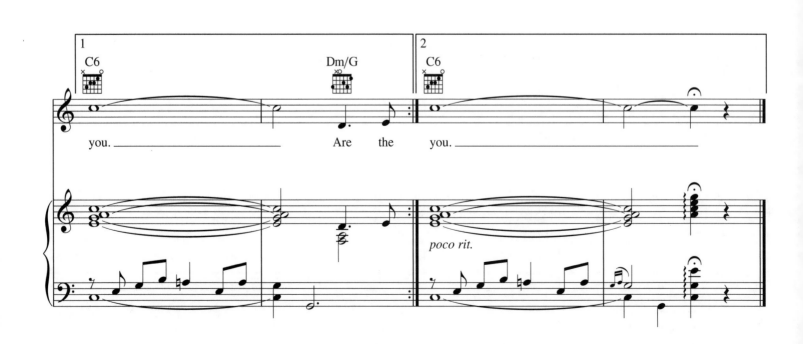

you. _____ Are the you. _____

I'LL KNOW
from GUYS AND DOLLS

By FRANK LOESSER

I'VE GOT YOUR NUMBER

from LITTLE ME

Music by CY COLEMAN
Lyrics by CAROLYN LEIGH

Moderate, with a relaxed swinging beat

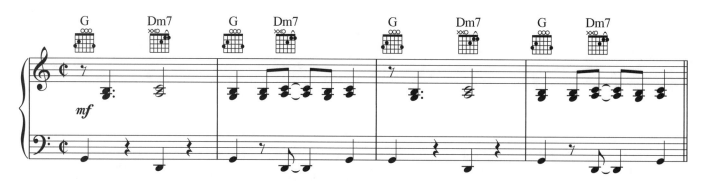

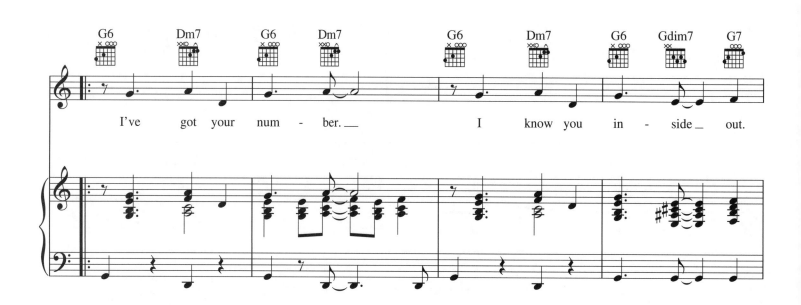

I've got your num - ber. ___ I know you in - side ___ out.

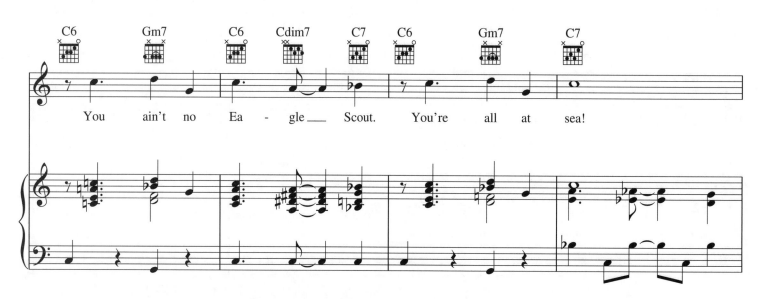

You ain't no Ea - gle ___ Scout. You're all at sea!

IF I ONLY HAD A BRAIN
from THE WIZARD OF OZ

Lyric by E.Y. "YIP" HARBURG
Music by HAROLD ARLEN

Scarecrow: Said a scare-crow swing-in' on a pole ___ to a black-bird sit-tin' on a
Tin Woodman: Said a tin-man rat-tlin' his ___ gibs ___ to a straw-man sad and wea-ry-
Cowardly Lion: Said a li-on, poor neu-rot-ic lion, ___ to a miss who lis-tened to him

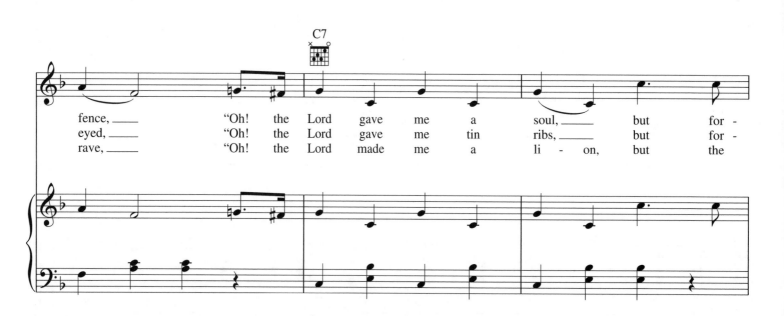

fence, ___ "Oh! the Lord gave me a soul, ___ but for-
eyed, ___ "Oh! the Lord gave me tin ribs, ___ but for-
rave, ___ "Oh! the Lord made me a li-on, but the

got to give me com - mon sense. ___ If I had an ounce of com - mon
got to put a heart in - side." ___ Then he banged his hol - low chest and
Lord for - got to make me brave." ___ Then his tail be - gan to curl and

Moderately

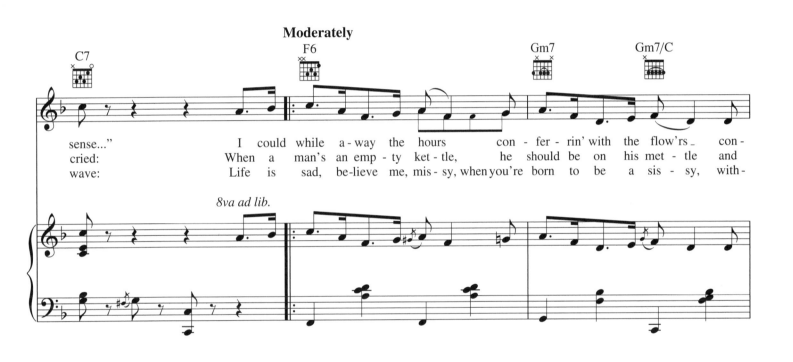

sense..." I could while a - way the hours con - fer - rin' with the flow'rs ___ con -
cried: When a man's an emp - ty ket - tle, he should be on his met - tle and
wave: Life is sad, be - lieve me, mis - sy, when you're born to be a sis - sy, with-

8va ad lib.

sult - in' with the rain. ___ And my head I'd be scratch - in' while my
yet I'm torn a - part. ___ Just be - cause I'm pre - sum - in' that I
out the vim and verve. ___ But I could change my hab - its, nev - er

loco   *3*

8va ad lib.

IF I WERE A BELL

from GUYS AND DOLLS

By FRANK LOESSER

IF THIS ISN'T LOVE

from FINIAN'S RAINBOW

Words by E.Y. "YIP" HARBURG
Music by BURTON LANE

Dm7 G7 C Dm G7 C
top of Will - iam Tell. With this I can - not grap - ple, be -
B7 Em D7 G7
D.S. al Coda
cause, be - cause you're so a - dor - a - belle. If
CODA
Cmaj7/G Cdim/E♭ Dm7 F/G G7
4fr
bust - in' with bliss, and I'll kiss your hand if this is - n't
C F C
love!
8va

ISN'T IT A PITY?

from PARDON MY ENGLISH

Music and Lyrics by GEORGE GERSHWIN
and IRA GERSHWIN

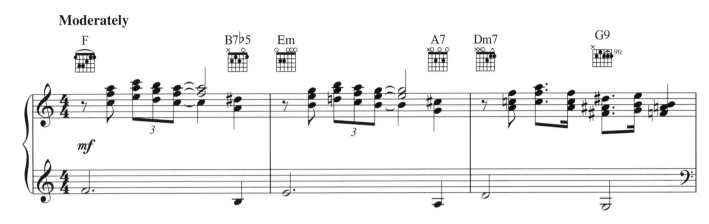

Michael: Why did I wan - der here and there and yon - der,
Ilse: While you were flit - ting I was bus - y knit - ting,

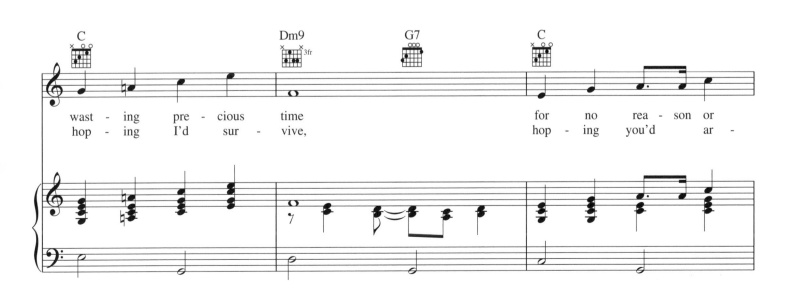

wast - ing pre - cious time for no rea - son or
hop - ing I'd sur - vive, hop - ing you'd ar -

164

IT AIN'T NECESSARILY SO

from PORGY AND BESS®

Music and Lyrics by GEORGE GERSHWIN,
DuBOSE and DOROTHY HEYWARD
and IRA GERSHWIN

IT'S DE-LOVELY
from RED, HOT AND BLUE!

Words and Music by
COLE PORTER

IT'S A GRAND NIGHT FOR SINGING

from STATE FAIR

Lyrics by OSCAR HAMMERSTEIN II
Music by RICHARD RODGERS

Tempo di Valse

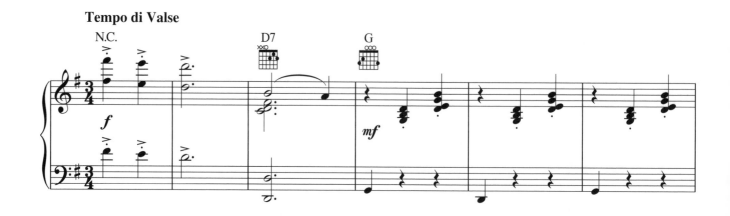

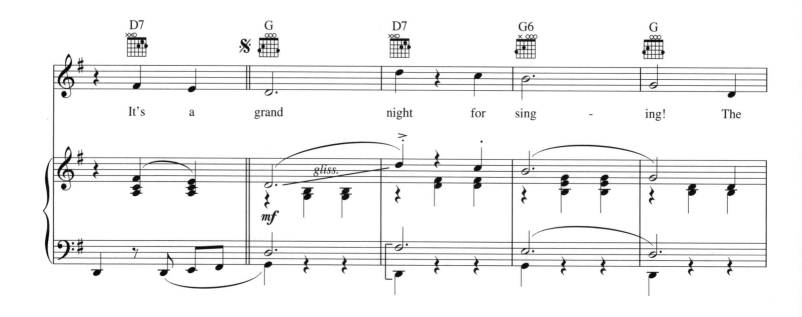

It's a grand night for sing - ing! The

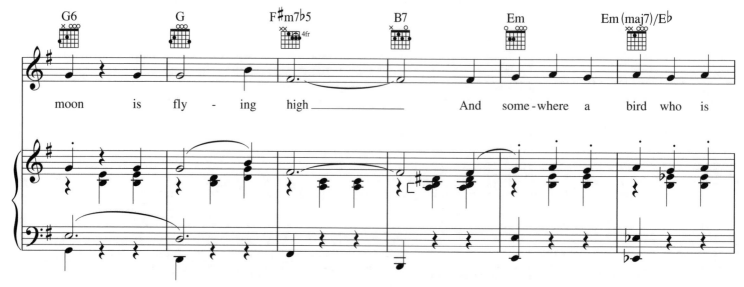

moon is fly - ing high _____ And some-where a bird who is

LOOK TO THE RAINBOW

from FINIAN'S RAINBOW

Words by E.Y. "YIP" HARBURG
Music by BURTON LANE

LUCKY TO BE ME
from ON THE TOWN

Words by BETTY COMDEN and ADOLPH GREEN
Music by LEONARD BERNSTEIN

LULLABY OF BROADWAY

from GOLD DIGGERS OF 1935
from 42ND STREET

Words by AL DUBIN
Music by HARRY WARREN

MACK THE KNIFE

from THE THREEPENNY OPERA

English Words by MARC BLITZSTEIN
Original German Words by BERT BRECHT
Music by KURT WEILL

MAKE SOMEONE HAPPY

from DO RE MI

Words by BETTY COMDEN and ADOLPH GREEN
Music by JULE STYNE

NAMELY YOU
from LI'L ABNER

Words by JOHNNY MERCER
Music by GENE DePAUL

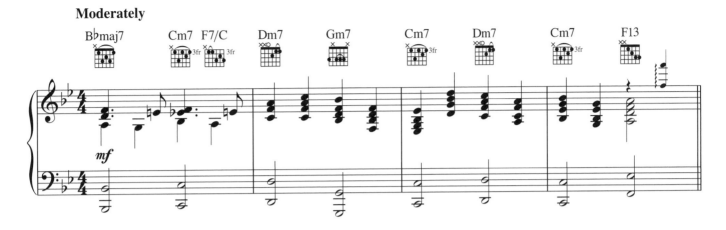

You de-serve a {gal/boy} who's will-in', _____ name-ly me.

One who'd love to raise your chil-lun, _____ name-ly me.

NEW YORK, NEW YORK

from ON THE TOWN

Lyrics by BETTY COMDEN and ADOLPH GREEN
Music by LEONARD BERNSTEIN

NICE WORK IF YOU CAN GET IT
from A DAMSEL IN DISTRESS

Music and Lyrics by GEORGE GERSHWIN
and IRA GERSHWIN

Lov - ing one who loves you, And then tak - ing that

vow, Nice work __ if you can get it, And if you

get it, __ Won't you tell me how?

how? __

OH, WHAT A BEAUTIFUL MORNIN'

from OKLAHOMA!

Lyrics by OSCAR HAMMERSTEIN II
Music by RICHARD RODGERS

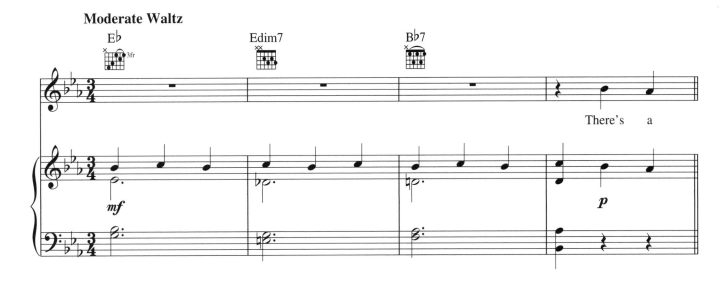

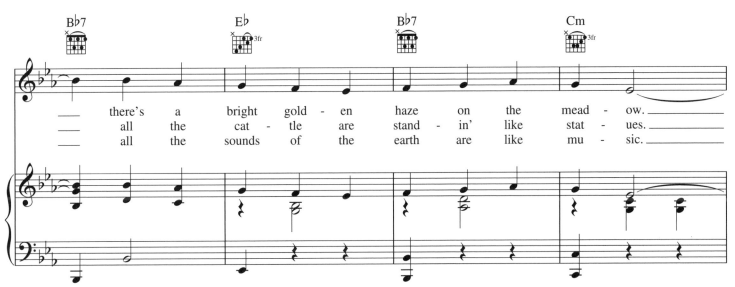

OH, LADY BE GOOD!

from the Broadway Musical LADY, BE GOOD!

Music and Lyrics by GEORGE GERSHWIN
and IRA GERSHWIN

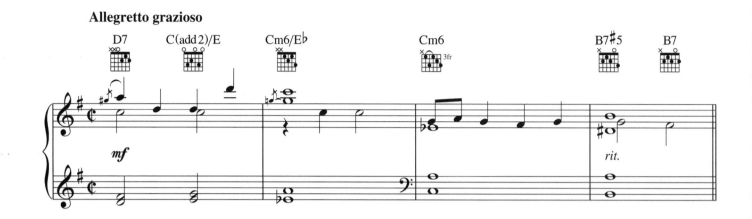

Listen to my tale of woe, It's ter-ri-bly sad, but
Au-burn and bru-nette and blonde: I love 'em all, tall or

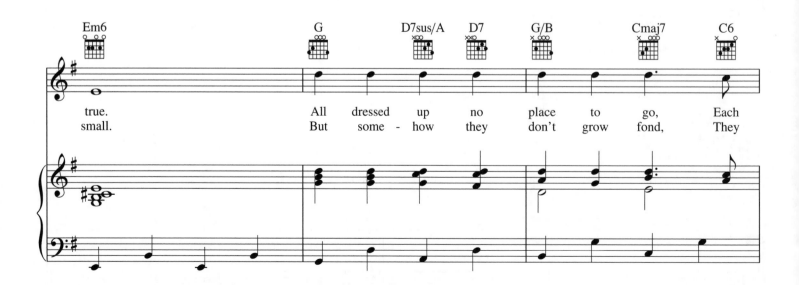

true. All dressed up no place to go, Each
small. But some-how no they don't grow fond, They

ON MY OWN

from LES MISÉRABLES

Music by CLAUDE-MICHEL SCHÖNBERG
Lyrics by ALAIN BOUBLIL, JEAN-MARC NATEL,
HERBERT KRETZMER, JOHN CAIRD
and TREVOR NUNN

220

OVER THE RAINBOW

from THE WIZARD OF OZ

Music by HAROLD ARLEN
Lyric by E.Y. "YIP" HARBURG

225

THE PARTY'S OVER
from BELLS ARE RINGING

Words by BETTY COMDEN and ADOLPH GREEN
Music by JULE STYNE

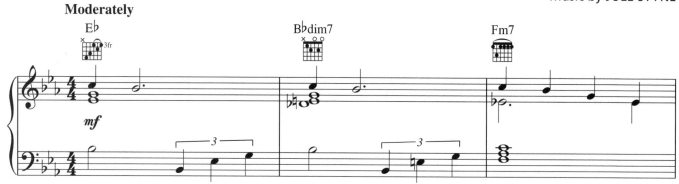

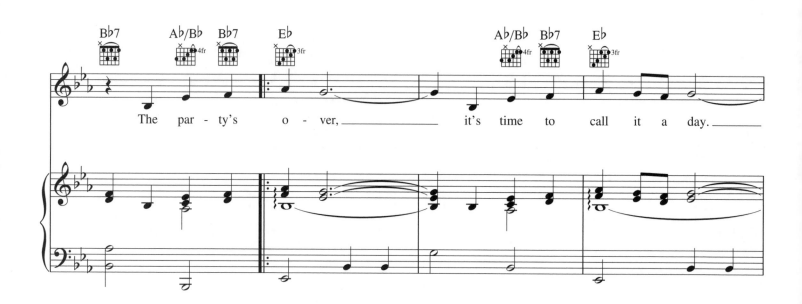

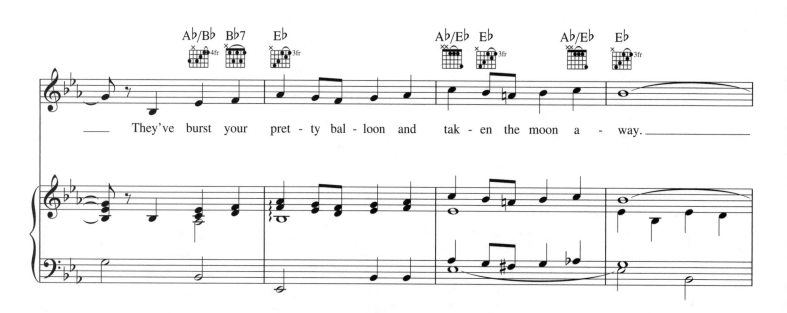

be-ing with him. _____ Now you must wake up, _____ all dreams must

end. _____ Take off your make-up, _____ the par-ty's

o-ver. _____ It's all o-ver, _____ my

friend. _____ The par-ty's friend. _____

Send in the Clowns

from the Musical A LITTLE NIGHT MUSIC

Words and Music by
STEPHEN SONDHEIM

'S WONDERFUL

from FUNNY FACE
from AN AMERICAN IN PARIS

Music and Lyrics by GEORGE GERSHWIN
and IRA GERSHWIN

Life has just be - gun.
Jack has found his Jill.
Don't mind tell - ing you, in my hum - ble fash,

Don't know what you've done, but I'm all a - thrill.
that you thrill me through with a ten - der pash.

How can words ex - press your di - vine ap - peal?
When you said you care, 'mag - ine my e - mosh.

SINGIN' IN THE RAIN

from SINGIN' IN THE RAIN

Lyric by ARTHUR FREED
Music by NACIO HERB BROWN

Fine

sing - in', ___ just sing - in' in ___ the rain. _____

Why am I smil - in' and why do I sing? ___

Why does De - cem - ber seem sun - ny as Spring? ___

Why do I get up each morn - ing to start _____

SOME OTHER TIME

from ON THE TOWN

Lyrics by BETTY COMDEN and ADOLPH GREEN
Music by LEONARD BERNSTEIN

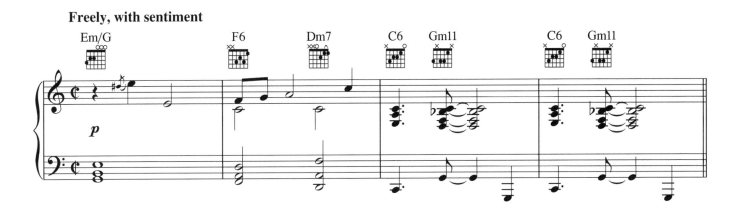

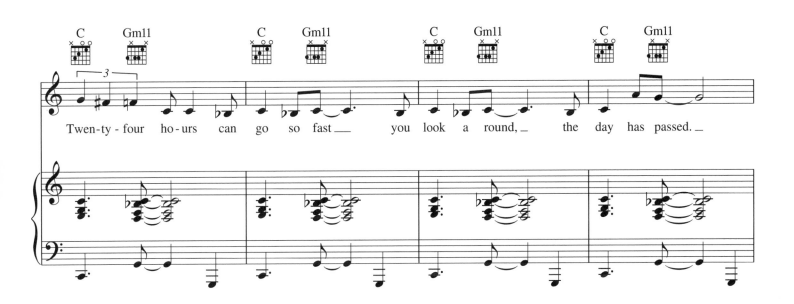

Twen-ty- four ho-urs can go so fast _ you look a round, _ the day has passed. _

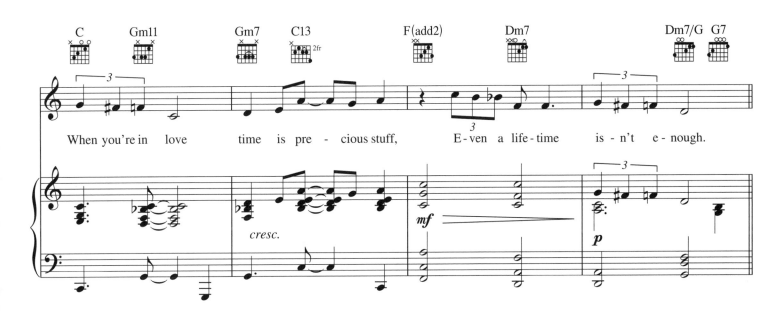

When you're in love time is pre - cious stuff, E-ven a life-time is - n't e - nough.

SMALL WORLD
from GYPSY

Words by STEPHEN SONDHEIM
Music by JULE STYNE

SOMEONE TO WATCH OVER ME

from OH, KAY!

Music and Lyrics by GEORGE GERSHWIN
and IRA GERSHWIN

There's a say-ing old Says that love is blind, Still we're of-ten told, "Seek and ye shall find." So I'm going to seek A cer-tain lad I've had in mind. Look-ing ev-'ry-where, Have-n't

THERE'S A BOAT DAT'S LEAVIN' SOON FOR NEW YORK

from PORGY AND BESS®

Music and Lyrics by
GEORGE GERSHWIN, IRA GERSHWIN,
DuBOSE and DOROTHY HEYWARD

Moderate Blues tempo

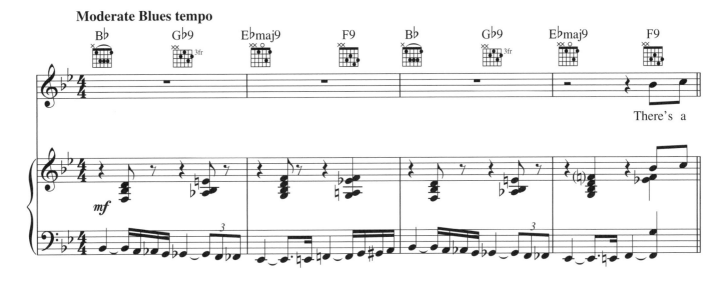

There's a

boat dat's leav-in' soon _ for New York, _

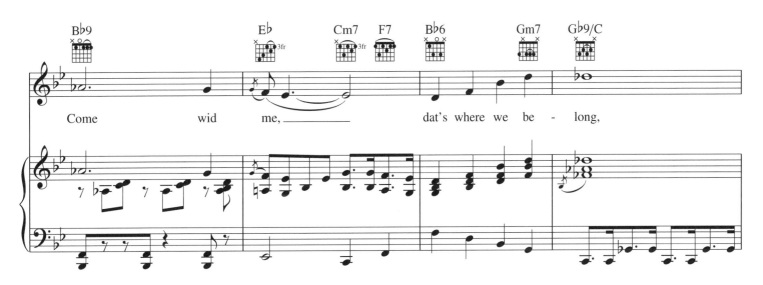

Come wid me, _ dat's where we be-long,

SUMMERTIME

from PORGY AND BESS®

Music and Lyrics by GEORGE GERSHWIN,
DuBOSE and DOROTHY HEYWARD
and IRA GERSHWIN

Moderately, with expression

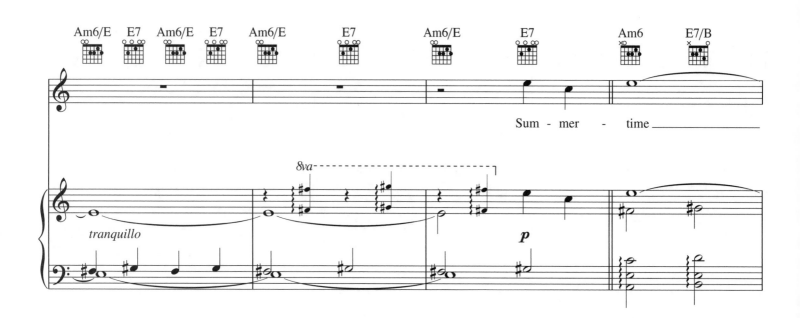

Sum - mer - time

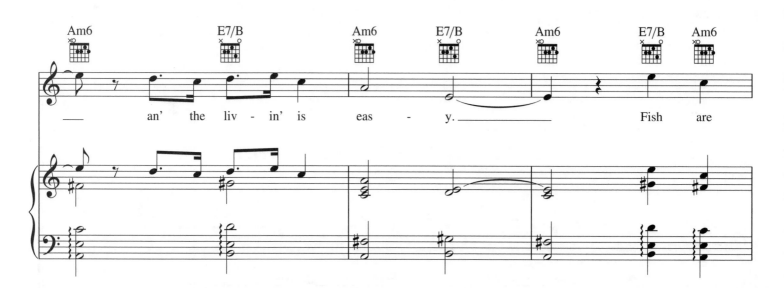

an' the liv - in' is eas - y. Fish are

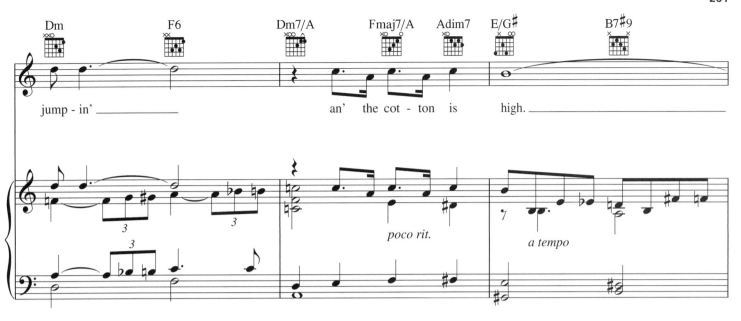

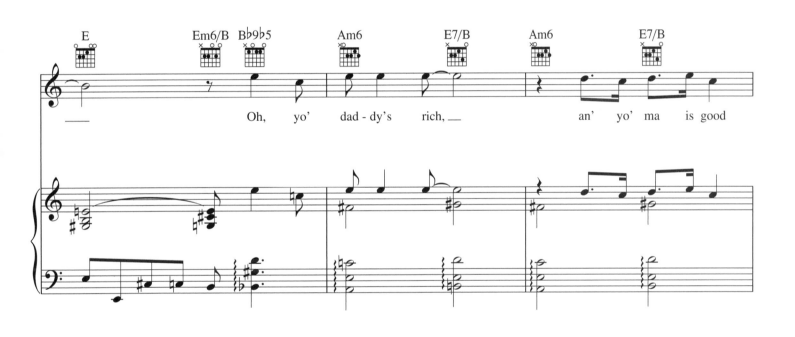

TOGETHER WHEREVER WE GO
from GYPSY

Words by STEPHEN SONDHEIM
Music by JULE STYNE

TWO LOST SOULS

from DAMN YANKEES

Words and Music by RICHARD ADLER
and JERRY ROSS

Moderately slow, with a heavy beat

Two lost souls on the high-way of life. We

ain't e-ven got a sis-ter or broth-er. ___ But ain't it just great,

ain't it just grand? We've got each oth-er! ___

WHY CAN'T YOU BEHAVE?

from KISS ME, KATE

Words and Music by
COLE PORTER

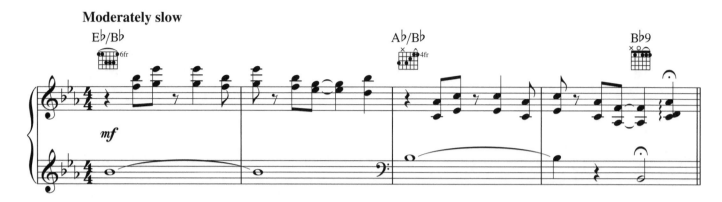

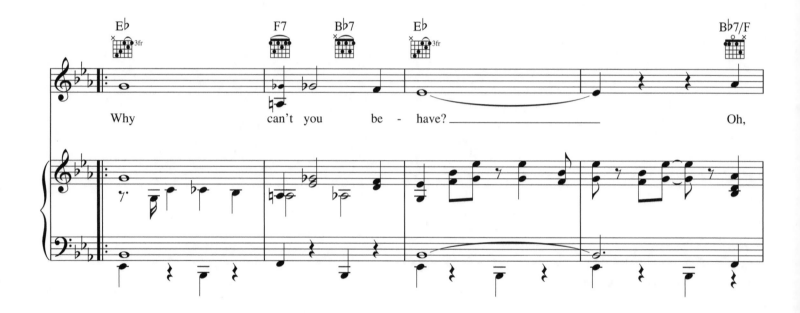

Why can't you be - have? _____ Oh,

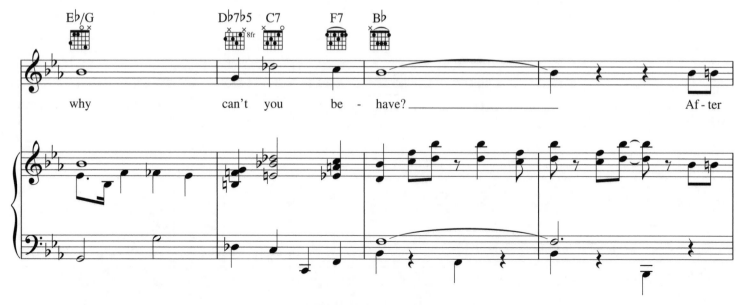

why can't you be - have? _____ Af - ter

WOULDN'T IT BE LOVERLY

from MY FAIR LADY

Lyrics by ALAN JAY LERNER
Music by FREDERICK LOEWE

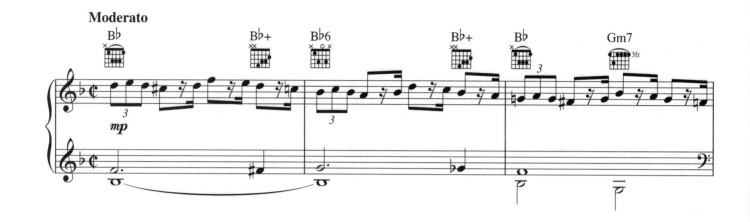

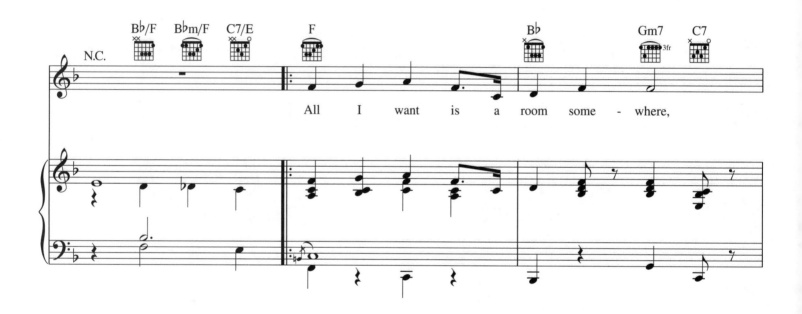

All I want is a room some-where,

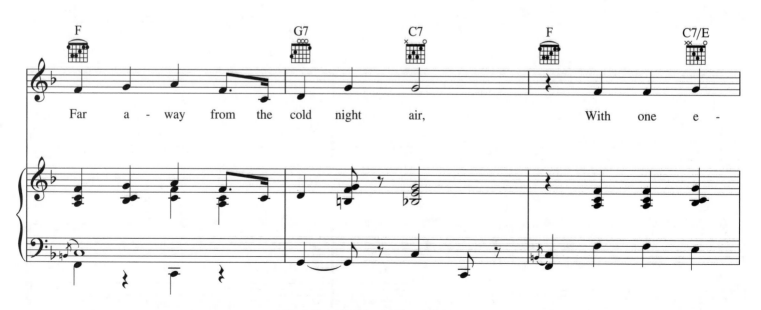

Far a-way from the cold night air, With one e-

YOU'RE GETTING TO BE A HABIT WITH ME

from 42ND STREET

Lyrics by AL DUBIN
Music by HARRY WARREN

YOUNG AND FOOLISH

from PLAIN AND FANCY

Words by ARNOLD B. HORWITT
Music by ALBERT HAGUE

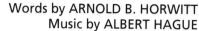

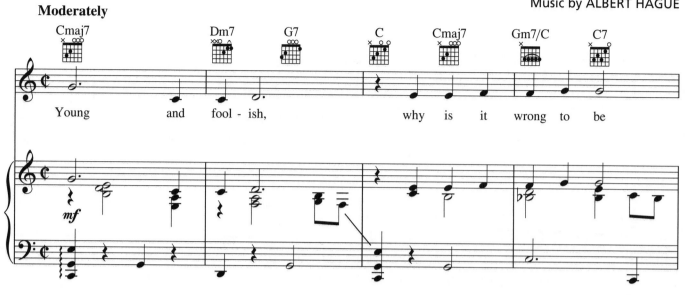

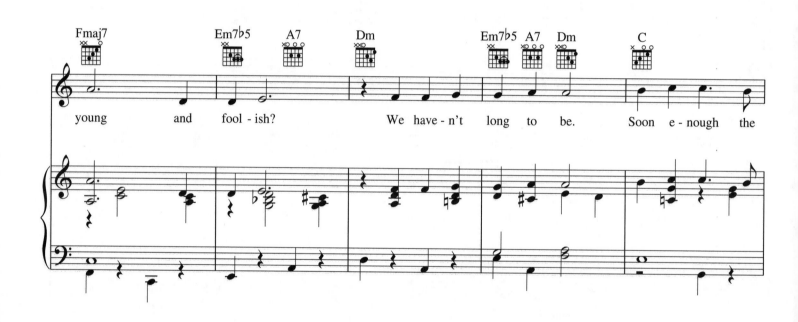

WHATEVER LOLA WANTS
(Lola Gets)
from DAMN YANKEES

Words and Music by RICHARD ADLER
and JERRY ROSS